That's *Switzerland*

Ein Bilderbuch
A picture book
Un livre d'images
写真集

*To Suzan + Larry —
in memory of a wonderful
week we spent together —
thank you for coming,
we hope to see you again!
Yvonne + Beat*

AT Verlag

Hettingen, 07 – 14 – 93

Die Schweiz

Die Schweiz – ein kleines Land mitten in Europa! Die Mitte Europas? Tatsächlich, denn das Land am Alpenkamm ist die Drehscheibe zwischen Nord und Süd, Ost und West. Vier Sprachen werden in diesem kleinen Land gesprochen: Deutsch, Französisch, Italienisch und Rätoromanisch. Vier Kulturen leben auf engem Raum friedlich zusammen und bereichern sich gegenseitig. So verschieden wie die Menschen, so mannigfaltig sind auch die Landschaften. Zerklüftete Schneeberge und unzugängliche Täler liegen unweit sanfter Seeufer, in deren mildem Klima sogar Palmen und Zypressen wachsen. So ist die Schweiz auch ein Europa im Kleinen. Weil das Land keine Rohstoffe besitzt, war der Erfindungsgeist seiner Bewohner seit jeher gross. Darum gibt es so viele Klischeevorstellungen rund um die Schweiz: Schokolade und Käse, Uhren und Schmuck, Banken und Franken sind Markenzeichen für die innovative Wirtschaft des Landes; Heidi, Alphorn und Matterhorn für die vielgestaltige Tradition und die herrliche Landschaft. Doch diese weltbekannten Begriffe allein machen die Schweiz nicht aus. Die moderne Schweiz ist ein zukunftsgerichtetes Land, das weiss, was es der intakten Natur in all ihrer Schönheit, seiner langen Geschichte und der Arbeitsleistung und Gastfreundschaft seiner Bevölkerung zu verdanken hat: Wohlstand und grosses Ansehen in der ganzen Welt.

Switzerland

Switzerland—the tiny country in the middle of Europe! The middle of Europe? Yes, indeed, for the country nestled on the ridge of the Alps is the cross-roads between north and south, between east and west. Four languages are spoken here: German, French, Italian and Rhaeto-Romanic. Four cultures peacefully share the country's tiny space and enhance each other. The diversity of Switzerland's peoples is also reflected in the contrasts of its landscape. Jagged, snowcapped mountains and inaccessible valleys are not far from gentle lakeshores, where even palms and cypresses thrive in the mild climate. Switzerland is Europe in miniature. As the country has no raw materials of its own, the inhabitants are all the more inventive. That's why Switzerland has so many clichés. Chocolate and cheese, watches and jewellery, banks and francs are the trademarks of the country's innovative economy; Heidi, alphorn and Matterhorn for its many-faceted tradition and magnificent landscape. Yet these world-renowned concepts alone do not define everything about Switzerland. Modern Switzerland is a progressive country, well aware of what its unspoilt nature in all its beauty, its long history, and the productivity and hospitality of its people has yielded; prosperity and prestige all over the world.

La Suisse

La Suisse – un petit pays au milieu de l'Europe! Est-elle le centre de l'Europe? Certainement, car ce pays à la frange des Alpes est la plaque tournante entre le nord et le sud, l'est et l'ouest. Dans ce petit territoire, on parle quatre langues: l'allemand, le français, l'italien et le romanche. Quatre cultures vivent en harmonie dans un espace restreint en s'enrichissant mutuellement. A la diversité des hommes répond la grande variété des paysages. Sommets neigeux et crevassés ne sont pas loin des rives douces d'un lac dont le climat permet la croissance de palmiers et de cyprès. La Suisse est ainsi l'image de l'Europe en modèle réduit. L'absence de matières premières dans son sous-sol stimule implicitement l'esprit inventif de ses habitants. C'est la raison pour laquelle tant de clichés circulent à propos de la Suisse: le chocolat et le fromage, les montres et les bijoux, les banques et l'argent sont les images de marque de l'économie du pays; Heidi, le cor des Alpes et le cervin le sont pour la tradition aux multiples facettes, ainsi que pour les merveilleux paysages. Pourtant ces concepts mondialement connus ne font pas toute la Suisse. La Suisse moderne se tourne vers le futur en étant consciente de ce qu'elle doit à la nature intacte dans toute sa beauté, à son riche passé ainsi qu'à l'esprit travailleur et hospitalier de ses habitants: le bien-être et une grande considération de par le monde.

スイス　序

スイス―それはヨーロッパの真中にある小国。ヨーロッパの真中ですって？その通り。アルプス山脈の土地柄、東西南北の中心にある回転盤のような所です。この小国ではドイツ語、フランス語、イタリア語、レートロマンシュ語と4つの国語が話されています。4つの文化が狭い中でも平和に共存し、相互に豊さを増しているのです。人が多様であるように風景も種々様々。穏やかな気候の故、ヤシやイトスギすらも生息する快い湖岸から程遠くもなく、峨々たる雪山や到達しがたい渓谷が横たわっています。こういったスイスはヨーロッパの縮小版でもあるわけです。国が資源を保有しない分、住民の独創力は豊か。そのせいかスイスにはたくさんのイメージが結びつけられています。チョコレート、チーズ、時計や装飾品、銀行にスイスフラン、これらは革新的経済のトレードマーク。ハイジ、アルペンホルンにマッターホルンと言えば色々な形での伝統や見事な景観。しかしこういった世界的に有名な概念だけでスイスができあがっているわけではありません。現代スイスは未来を志向する国。その裕福さと世界における大いなる信望、それが何のおかげであるのかを知っている国です。損なわれぬ自然、とりわけその美しさ、長い歴史、国民の労働能率やホスピタリティー。

Highlights
ハイライト

Das Matterhorn, der bekannteste und spektakulärste Alpengipfel.

The Matterhorn, the best known and most spectacular alpine peak.

Le Cervin, sommet le plus connu et le plus spectaculaire des Alpes.

マッターホルン。最も有名で壮観なアルプスの頂。

Highlights

Das Matterhorn! Klar, der schönste Berg der Welt. Den muss man einfach gesehen haben! So denken viele Touristen. Und auch die Werbung bedient sich des markanten Alpengipfels immer wieder, zeigt vor dem kantigen Berg Uhren, Schmuck, Schokolade und manch anderes. Da muss tatsächlich was dran sein an diesem Berg. Das Matterhorn ist eben kein gewöhnlicher Berg: Ganz für sich allein ragt er in den Himmel, zeigt sich nur dem, der die Reise nach Zermatt auf sich nimmt. Geheimnisse ranken sich um seine Erstbesteigung.

Highlights haben meist etwas Erhabenes, Grosses, Mysteriöses an sich. Die Aareschlucht bei Meiringen ist wegen Sherlock Holmes' Todessturz berühmt, das Jungfraujoch durch die kühn in die Eigernordwand gehauene Zahnradbahn und das überwältigende Panorama auf Gletscher, Gipfel und Mittelland. Der Name der Städte Zürich, Luzern und Genf hat etwas Glamouröses an sich, sei es wegen ihrer tollen Geschäfte, wegen ihrer Geschichte oder einfach wegen ihrer unvergleichlichen Lage am See. Bern ist weniger berühmt als Regierungssitz, sondern vielmehr weil es eine der schönsten Altstädte Europas besitzt. Weitere Highlights? Das trutzige Kleinstädtchen Gruyères mit der Schaukäserei, der mächtige Rheinfall bei Schaffhausen, Lugano und Ascona in ihrer südlichen Umgebung... Doch trotz aller klingender Namen – welches Schweizer Reiseziel ist eigentlich kein Highlight?

Highlights

The Matterhorn! Without a doubt the world's most beautiful mountain and an absolute must! Many tourists would agree. Watches, jewellery, chocolate and many other items are advertised again and again against the dramatic backdrop of this unique alpine peak. There is something very special about the Matterhorn. It is indeed no ordinary mountain: standing alone, it reaches up into the heavens, revealing itself only for those who make their way to Zermatt. Its first conquest is steeped in secrecy!

There is usually something grand about highlights, something great and mysterious. The Aare Gorge near Meiringen became famous when Sherlock Holmes fell to his death. The Jungfraujoch has the rack railway, cut boldly into the Eiger's North Wall, and the overwhelming panoramic view of glaciers, peaks and the Mittelland area. The cities Zurich, Lucerne and Geneva have a glamorous ring: is it their choice of shops, their history or simply their unrivalled lakeshore locations? Bern is famous, not as the country's capital, but for its old city, Europe's most beautiful. More highlights? How about the defiant little town of Gruyères, with its dairy, the mighty Rhine Falls near Schaffhausen, Lugano and Ascona in their southern settings... All this grandeur aside—what spot in Switzerland isn't a highlight, anyway?

Highlights

Le Cervin! Certes la plus belle montagne du monde. Bien des touristes pensent qu'il est indispensable de l'avoir vu! Et la publicité ne se fait pas faute d'utiliser encore et toujours ce sommet alpin caractéristique comme toile de fond pour des montres, des bijoux, du chocolat et bien d'autres choses. Le Cervin n'est pas un sommet ordinaire: tout seul, il s'élance vers le ciel et ne se montre qu'à celui qui a entrepris le voyage à Zermatt. Bien des mystères entourent sa première ascension!

Les figures tutélaires sont la plupart du temps auréolées de majesté, de grandeur, de mystère. Les gorges de l'Aar près de Meiringen doivent leur célébrité à la chute mortelle de Sherlock Holmes, le Jungfraujoch à son train à crémaillère audacieusement accroché à la paroi nord de l'Eiger ainsi qu'à son panorama époustouflant sur les glaciers et les montagnes. L'évocation des noms de villes telles Zurich, Lucerne et Genève a quelque chose de prestigieux en raison de leurs magasins haut de gamme, leur passé historique ou simplement leur situation incomparable au bord d'un lac. Berne est moins connue pour sa fonction de siège du gouvernement que pour sa vieille ville considérée comme l'une des plus belles d'Europe. Que citer d'autre parmi les symboles de la Suisse? La petite ville fortifiée de Gruyères avec sa fromagerie, les magnifiques chutes du Rhin à Schaffhouse, Lugano et Ascona dans leur cadre méridional... Mais au fond, quelle destination, en Suisse, n'est-elle pas un *highlight*?

ハイライト

マッターホルン！勿論、世界で一番美しい山。とにかく見てみなくてはならない。そう思う観光客は多勢でしょう。この抜きんでたアルプスの頂は広告にも繰り返し使われており、時計、宝石類、チョコレート、その他多くの物が、尖った山の前に並んでいます。実際この山には何かがあるにちがいない。そう、マッターホルンはただの山ではありません。一峰だけが天へと聳え立ち、ツェルマットまで自ら足を運ぶ者にのみその姿を見せてくれます。その初登頂は曰く付き。だいたいハイライトというものには何か高揚した、偉大な、神秘的なことがつきもの。マイリンゲンのアレ渓谷はシャーロック・ホームズが転落死した地として有名ですし、ユングフラウヨッホはアイガー北壁を大胆に切り抜いた中を走る登山列車や氷河、山々の頂、ミッテルランドに広がる圧巻のパノラマでお馴染。また、チューリッヒ、ルッツェルン、ジュネーヴといった町の名には何か魅惑的な響きがあります。素敵な店とか歴史とか、それとも単に比類なき湖岸にあるといったように。ベルンは首都としてよりヨーロッパの美しい古都の一つとして知られています。さらにハイライトを挙げてみましょうか？チーズ作りを披露する誇り高き小さな町グリュイエール、シャフハウゼンの力強きラインの滝、南国風なルガノやアスコーナ…。色々浮かび上がる所はあるけれど、ハイライトにならないスイスの旅先って一体どこでしょう？

Luzern. Die Kapell-
brücke – innen mit
Totentanzbildern
verziert – und der
mächtige Wasser-
turm vor der Altstadt.

Lucerne. The Chapel
Bridge with its
«Danse Macabre»
paintings inside and
the mighty water
tower by the Old
Town.

Lucerne. Le Pont de
la Chapelle, décoré
intérieurement de
scènes de la danse
des morts, et l'impo-
sante Tour d'eau
devant la vieille ville.

ルッツェルン。旧市街を
背景に、死者の踊りの絵
画等で内装されたカペル
橋と水塔（ヴァッサート
ゥルム）。

Lugano. Palmengesäumte Seeufer und der markante Felsen des Monte San Salvatore.

Lugano. Palm-lined lakeshores and the striking cliffs of the Monte San Salvatore.

Lugano. Palmiers en bordure du lac et le rocher caractéristique du Mont San Salvatore.

ルガノ。ヤシの木に縁取られた湖岸、南国調の暮らし、サン・サルヴァトーレ山の独特な岩。

Bern. In einer Flussschleife gelegen, wird die Hauptstadt der Schweiz vom Münster überragt.

Bern. Situated in a river's bend, Switzerland's capital city is towered over by the Cathedral.

Berne. Située dans un méandre de l'Aare, la capitale de la Suisse est dominée par sa cathédrale.

ベルン。川が一くねりした所に位置するスイスの首都。ゴシック様式大寺院が聳える。

Schloss Chillon bei
Montreux am Gen-
fersee. Die Dents du
Midi (3257 m) sind
Ausläufer der Wal-
liser Hochalpen.

The Chillon Castle
near Montreux
on Lake Geneva.
The Dents du Midi
(3257 m) form the
foothills of the Valais
Alps.

Le Château
de Chillon près de
Montreux au bord
du lac Léman.
Au fond, les Dents
du Midi (3257 m),
dernier sommet
des hautes Alpes
valaisannes.

レマン湖畔、モントルー
のシヨン城。ダン・デュ
ミディ（3257 m）は
ヴァレ・アルプスの支脈。

Das Land
The country
Le pays
国土

Bielersee mit
der St.-Peters-Insel.
Über dem Winzer-
dorf Ligerz steht die
Kirche Heilig Kreuz
inmitten von Reb-
bergen.

Lake Biel and
St. Peter's Island.
In the heart of
vineyards above the
wine-growing village
of Ligerz stands the
Holy Cross Church.

Le lac de Bienne et
l'île St-Pierre.
Au-dessus du village
vigneron de Ligerz se
dresse l'église de la
Sainte Croix au
milieu des vignobles.

サンクト・ペーター半島
とビール湖。葡萄栽培の
村リゲルツ上方、葡萄地
の真中には、聖十字教会
が立つ。

Das Land

Verschiedenste Landschaftsformen sind in der Schweiz auf engstem Raum vereint. Die Alpen sind das mächtige Rückgrat, durchzogen von einer Vielzahl grosser und kleiner Täler. Diese haben oft ein ganz eigenes Klima, denn der Föhn, ein warmer Fallwind, bringt bisweilen für Tage warmes und sonniges Wetter. Südlich der Alpen sind Klima und Vegetation vorwiegend mediterran. Das Tessin öffnet sich hier zögernd gegen die weite Poebene. Im Norden liegt das dichtbesiedelte, fruchtbare Mittelland. Es ist geprägt von Städten und Dörfern, Hügelzügen, Seen und Wasserläufen. Der Jura im Nordwesten besteht aus mehreren sanften, langgezogenen Bergzügen. Hier weiden Pferde auf den Wiesen, hier versickert alles Wasser in den kalkhaltigen Boden, um sich in den Seen am Jurafuss wieder zu sammeln. Die Landschaften der Schweiz wurden vor langer Zeit von Gletschern geschaffen. Wind, Wetter und Wasser haben ihnen ihr heutiges Aussehen gegeben. Der Mensch hat seine Umwelt durch Akkerbau, Industrie, Verkehr und Wohnungsbau geprägt. Land- und Viehwirtschaft werden in der Schweiz nicht nur in fruchtbaren ehemaligen Sumpfgebieten wie dem Berner Seeland getrieben, sondern überall, wo es Boden und Klima erlauben: an den steilen Hügeln des Emmentals, an den von der Sonne versengten Hängen des Wallis und Graubündens und auf hoch in den Bergen gelegenen Alpweiden, die nur wenige Wochen nutzbar sind.

The Country

The most diverse landscapes meet in Switzerland's narrow confines. The powerful backbone of the Alps is criss-crossed with a multitude of big and little valleys. These often have their very own climates, for the *Föhn,* a warm fall wind, brings days of warm, sunny weather. South of the Alps, where Ticino reluctantly opens to the broad Po Valley, the climate and vegetation are mainly Mediterranean. To the north lies the fertile and heavily-populated Mittelland area, with its characteristic cities, villages, hills, lakes and water-courses. The Jura in the northwest is formed by several gentle, elongated mountains. Horses graze in the meadows and all the water trickles into the chalky ground to collect in the lakes at the foot of the Jura. A long time ago Switzerland's landscape was carved by glaciers. Wind, weather and water have made it what it is today. Man has made his mark on his environment with farming, industry, traffic and housing. But crop and stock farming is not restricted to the once marshy, fertile areas of the Bernese Seeland. Land is farmed wherever the soil and the climate will allow it: on the steep hills of the Emmental, on the sun-drenched slopes of the Valais and the Grisons, and even on alpine pastures high up in the mountains for the few weeks a year when this is possible.

Le pays

En Suisse, les paysages les plus divers se trouvent réunis dans un espace extrêmement restreint. Les Alpes en sont la majestueuse colonne vertébrale striée de petites et grandes vallées. Certaines d'entre elles jouissent d'un climat particulier dû au foehn, ce vent qui surgit brusquement et apporte pour quelques jours un temps beau et chaud. Au sud des Alpes, le climat et la végétation sont de type méditerranéen. Le Tessin s'ouvre discrètement vers la vaste plaine du Pô. Au nord se trouve le Moyen-Pays fertile et très peuplé, parsemé de villes et villages, de collines, de lacs et de cours d'eau. Au nord-ouest s'étend le Jura faisant ondoyer en douceur ses longues chaînes montagneuses. Des chevaux pâturent sur ses prés accueillants. Les eaux s'infiltrent dans son sol calcaire pour se répandre plus bas dans les lacs à ses pieds. Il y a fort longtemps, les grandes glaciations modelèrent les paysages, puis le vent, les intempéries et l'eau leur donnèrent leur aspect actuel. L'homme aussi laissa son empreinte dans son environnement par les cultures, l'industrie, les voies de communication et la construction. L'élevage et la culture ne se pratiquent pas uniquement dans les régions fertiles comme le Seeland bernois, mais aussi partout où le climat et le sol le permettent: sur les collines pentues de l'Emmental, les coteaux roussis par le soleil du Valais et des Grisons ainsi que les alpages situés très haut dans les montagnes, dont l'exploitation ne dure que quelques semaines en été.

国土

スイスという小さい面積の中には多様な景観が収まっています。アルプス山脈は強大な脊柱で、その間を縫って幾つもの大小様々な谷が広がります。こういった谷にはよく特別な気候状態があり、フェーンと呼ばれる暖かな風のために数日間暖かく晴れた天気が続くこともあります。アルプスの南側では気候や植物生育状況は主に地中海式で、ティチーノ地方は広いポー平野への入口になっています。アルプス北側には入植者の多い肥沃なミッテルランド。町や村、連なる丘陵、湖や水路に形造られています。また、北西に位置するユラ地方は多くの滑らかに尾を引く山並みから成り、ここでは馬が放牧され、水はカルキ分の強い土地にすっかり吸収され地下水となり、また後でユラ山麓の湖に集合することになります。ずっと以前に氷河によって形成されたスイスの景観は、風や天候、水により今日のような姿になってきました。人間は耕作、産業、交通、住居のために自らの環境を築いてきました。農牧業はスイスではベルンの湖水地方のような肥沃なかつての沼地帯でのみならず、土地と気候が許す限りどこででも行われています。エメンタールの急な丘陵でもヴァリスやグラウビュンデンの日に焦がされた斜面でも、また、僅か数週間しか使えない高い山の上、アルプの草原ででも。

Typisch für das
Appenzellerland sind
die weit über die
hügelige Landschaft
verstreuten Bauern-
häuser.

Farmhouses scat-
tered far and wide
over the rolling
countryside:
a typical Appenzell
scene.

Les fermes dissémi-
nées sur les nom-
breuses collines
appenzelloises sont
typiques de cette
région.

農家が散在するアッペン
ツェル地方の典型的な丘
陵地風景。

18

Das Lauteraarhorn spiegelt sich im Grimselstausee.

The Lauteraarhorn reflected in the Grimsel Reservoir.

Le Lauteraarhorn se reflète dans le lac artificiel du Grimsel.

グリムゼル貯水湖に反映
する、ラウテルアール氷
河を擁するラウテルアー
ルホルン。

Lange Hügelzüge und fruchtbare Täler prägen den Jura. Hier Bärschwil im Solothurner Jura.

Long rolling hills and fertile valleys are characteristic of the Jura. Bärschwil in Solothurn's Jura region.

Collines ondoyantes et vallées fertiles caractérisent le Jura. Ici Bärschwil dans le Jura soleurois.

連なる丘陵と肥沃な谷に
形造られるユラ地方。桜
の季節のソロトゥルン・
ユラ地方ベルシュヴィル。

Emmental. Von diesen Hügeln, wo die Hausdächer fast bis zum Boden reichen, stammt der berühmteste Schweizer Käse.

Emmental. The famous Swiss cheese comes from these hills, where the roofs almost reach the ground.

Emmental. Le fromage suisse le plus réputé provient de ces collines où les toits des maisons descendent presque jusqu'au sol.

エメンタール。屋根が地面に届くほどの家が立つこの丘陵地帯で、有名なスイスのチーズは生まれる。

23

Städte
Cities
Les villes
町

Zürich. Neben dem Fraumünster zeugen behäbige Stadthäuser von Reichtum und Selbstverständnis der Bürger.

Zurich. The Minster and sedate town houses reflect the wealth and pride of its citizens.

Zurich. A côté du Fraumünster les maisons cossues témoignent de l'opulence et du prestige des bourgeois.

チューリッヒ。フラウミュンスター（聖母寺院）のそばに並ぶどっしりとした家並は、市民の豊さや自信を示す。

Städte

Die typische Schweizer Stadt, ob gross oder klein, liegt am Wasser. Dies ist nicht erstaunlich, waren doch die Wasserwege, Seen wie Flüsse, immer schon Handelsrouten. Und wer den Handel kontrollierte, bekam Einfluss und wurde zum natürlichen Zentrum für das weitere Umland. Zürich, Genf, Luzern und Thun liegen günstig und geschützt am Ende eines Sees. Die Seehäfen Lausanne, Neuenburg oder Rapperswil wurden zu Umladestationen für den regionalen Handel. Anders die Zähringerstädte Bern und Freiburg: Sie wurden von Adligen als Brückenstädte geplant und stiegen wie auch Basel zu Macht auf, weil sie wichtige Flussübergänge mit lukrativen Zolleinnahmen beherrschten. Dasselbe galt für Orte an den grossen Passstrassen: Brig, Bellinzona, Chur. Die grossen Ausnahmen sind St. Gallen und Sitten, die sich um religiöse Zentren bildeten, um das Kloster und den Bischofssitz. Die moderne Schweizer Stadt hat sich weit über den historischen Kern ausgebreitet. Dennoch bleibt die Altstadt das unbestrittene Zentrum mit attraktiven Geschäften, gemütlichen Restaurants und Hotels, einladenden Wohnhäusern und idyllischen Ecken und Gassen. Die Altstadt ist nicht Kulisse. In ihr vermengt sich die Geschichte mit der Dynamik und Lebensfreude der Gegenwart. Fantasievolle Neubauten und ein gut ausgebautes öffentliches Verkehrsnetz unterstreichen dies.

Cities

Typical Swiss cities, whether big or small, are situated near water. This is not surprising, as water-courses, lakes and rivers have always served as trade routes. The city controlling the trade gains influence and becomes the natural centre of the surrounding area. Zurich, Geneva, Lucerne and Thun each enjoy favourable and protected locations at the end of a lake. The lake ports of Lausanne, Neuchatel and Rapperswil became transfer stations for commerce in their region. Not so for the Zähringer cities of Bern and Fribourg: the Aristrocracy planned these as toll cities. Like Basel they rose to power, because lucrative tolls were collected on the important river crossings in their command. The same was true for locations on the pass roads: Brig, Bellinzona, Chur. Two important exceptions are St. Gall and Sion, which grew as religious centres around their monastery and bishopric. Modern Switzerland has long burst the bounds of its historical core. Yet the old cities remain the uncontested centres, with attractive shops, cozy restaurants and hotels, inviting dwellings and idyllic nooks and laneways. The old city is not just scenery. Here history blends with the dynamism and élan of the present as evident in the imaginative new buildings and efficient public transport systems.

Les villes

La ville typiquement suisse, qu'elle soit grande ou petite, se situe au bord de l'eau. Ce n'est pas étonnant puisque de tous temps lacs et fleuves étaient des voies commerciales. Le contrôle du commerce impliquait influence et autorité sur une région. Zurich, Genève, Lucerne et Thoune occupent des sites favorables et protégés au bout d'un lac. Les ports lacustres de Lausanne, Neuchâtel ou Rapperswil devinrent des stations de transbordement pour le commerce régional. Il en alla autrement pour les villes des Zaehringen Bern et Fribourg: planifiées comme villes-ponts par la noblesse, elles devinrent puissantes, tout comme Bâle, parce qu'elles contrôlaient d'importants passages fluviaux grevés de taxes douanières fort lucratives. Les villes situées sur les routes des grands cols connurent le même essor, telles Brigue, Bellinzone et Coire. St-Gall et Sion sont les grandes exceptions puisqu'elles doivent leur développement à des hauts-lieux de la religion: St-Gall à son célèbre monastère et Sion au fait qu'elle est le siège de l'épiscopat. La ville moderne suisse s'est toujours développée autour de son noyau historique qui en reste cependant le centre incontesté avec ses commerces, ses restaurants, ses hôtels, ses maisons accueillantes et ses ruelles aux recoins idylliques. Dans la vieille ville l'histoire se mêle à la joie de vivre et au dynamisme du présent. Ses constructions modernes pleines de fantaisie et un réseau de transports en commun bien élaboré en complètent le tableau.

町

大きくとも小さくとも典型的なスイスの町といえば水際にあります。水路、湖、河川がもうずっと以前から商業取引ルートであったことを思えば、これは別に驚くに値しません。交易を取りしきる者が影響力を持ち周囲に広がる地域の中心となったのは当然の成り行きでしょう。チューリッヒ、ジュネーヴ、ルッツェルン、トゥーンは皆、有利な保護された湖の先端に位置しています。ローザンヌ、ヌシャテル、ラッペルスヴィルの港は地方交易の積み替え駅でした。他には、ツェーリング家の町であるベルンやフリブール。貴族達によって二つの町は橋渡しの町として計画され、バーゼルと同様、重要な川越えを司り高い税収入を得て、力を持つようになりました。同様なことが大きな峠のある地、ブリーク、ベリンツォーナ、クール、といった所にも当てはまります。大きな例外といえば、サンクト・ガレンとシッテン。これらの町は修道院と司教管区首都を取り巻き、宗教的中心地となりました。現代スイスの町は歴史的な中核からは更に広がっていますが、それでも尚、魅力的な店、居心地良いレストランやホテル、心引き付けられる住居や心なごむ街角、小路、といったもので、旧市街は今も明らかに中心として残っています。旧市街は見せ掛けだけの舞台装置ではありません。そこでは歴史が現在のダイナミックな力や生活の喜びと混ざりあっています。ファンタジー溢れる新建築物やよく拡張された公共交通網がこの点を際立たせています。

Berns Altstadt mit kopfsteingepflasterten Gassen und verwinkelten Dächern gehört zu den besterhaltenen Europas.

Bern's Old Town with its cobblestone lanes and patchwork roofs is among the best preserved in Europe.

La vieille ville de Berne aux ruelles pavées et pignons multiformes est l'une des mieux conservées d'Europe.

石畳の小道やギザギザ屋根の多いベルン旧市街はヨーロッパで最もよく保存された一郭。

Genf. Wahrzeichen
sind der UNO-Sitz
und der Jet d'Eau,
der höchste
Springbrunnen
der Schweiz.

Geneva. Landmarks
are the UN Head-
quarters and the Jet
d'Eau, the highest
fountain in Switzer-
land.

Genève. Le siège de
l'ONU et le jet d'eau
le plus haut de Suisse
sont les symboles de
cette ville.

ジュネーヴ。国際都市の
象徴である国連欧州本部
とスイス一高く吹き上げ
る大噴水。

Stein am Rhein,
sehenswert wegen
seiner kunstvollen
Erker und bunt
bemalten Hausfas-
saden.

Its artistic bay win-
dows and colourfully
painted façades
make Stein am Rhein
well worth a visit.

Stein am Rhein,
renommée pour ses
encorbellements
artistiques et ses
façades peintes.

シュタイン・アム・ライ
ン。芸術的な出窓や色彩
豊かに描かれた家のファ
ッサードが美しい小町。

30

St. Gallen. Der
barocke Neubau des
berühmten mittel-
alterlichen Klosters
stammt aus dem
18. Jahrhundert.

St. Gall. The
baroque reconstruc-
tion of this famous
medieval cloister
originates in the 18th
century.

St-Gall. La recon-
struction baroque du
célèbre monastère
médiéval date
du 18ᵉ siècle.

サンクト・ガレン。有名
な中世の修道院は、１８
世紀にバロック様式に建
て替えられた。

Berge
Mountains
Les montagnes
山

Eiger, Mönch und Jungfrau überragen, von ewigem Schnee bedeckt, die Hügel des Berner Mittellandes.

Towered over by the Eiger, Mönch and Jungfrau peaks and covered in eternal snow are the hills of Bern's Central Plateau.

L'Eiger, le Mönch et la Jungfrau, couverts de neige éternelle, dominent les collines du Moyen Pays bernois.

ベルナー・ミッテルランドの丘陵から抜きんでる、万年雪に被われたアイガー、メンヒ、ユングフラウ。

Berge

Gäbe es die Schweiz ohne Berge? Kaum! Seit Urzeiten überquerten Händler, Soldaten und Reisende die Alpen, die mächtige Barriere zwischen Nord- und Südeuropa. Hannibals Elefanten und Napoleons Heere, deutsche Kaiser und Dichter nahmen die beschwerlichen Saumpfade nach Italien unter die Füsse. Ohne die Alpentäler als Zuflucht und ohne Einkünfte aus dem Transitverkehr hätte es wohl nie einen eigenständigen Staat Schweiz gegeben. Die Berge selber jedoch kamen den Menschen immer bedrohlich vor. Unzählige Sagen beschreiben die Furcht vor den übermächtigen und unheilbringenden Naturkräften der Berge: von Felsstürzen, Lawinen, Sturm und Dämonen ist die Rede. Erst die spektakuläre Besteigung des Matterhorns durch den englischen Gipfelstürmer Edward Whymper 1865 und die Entdeckung der unberührten Bergwelt durch britische Touristen führten bei den Einheimischen zum Umdenken. Aus Bergdörfern wurden Höhenkurorte und mondäne Ferienzentren. Strassen, Bahnen und Lifte erschliessen heute Täler und Höhen. Wuchtige Talsperren zeugen von der Bedeutung der Wasserkraft für die Energieversorgung des Landes. Die europäischen Handelsströme führen durch die Alpentunnels. Trotz wirtschaftlicher Entwicklung bleibt den Schweizern aber ein oberstes Gebot: die Erhaltung des naturgegebenen Lebensraumes in seiner ganzen Schönheit — denn ohne diesen gäbe es die Schweiz nicht.

Mountains

Would there be a Switzerland without its mountains? Not likely! In early times, traders, soldiers and travellers crossed the Alps, the mighty barrier between Northern and Southern Europe. Hannibal's elephants and Napoleon's armies ventured the arduous mountain trails to Italy. Without the refuge of its alpine valleys and the income made from transit movement, the independent state of Switzerland would probably never have evolved. Yet the mountains showed a menacing face to the people. Legends abound describing the fear of their baneful, almighty powers: one spoke of rock-slides, avalanches, storms and demons. The spectacular conquest of the Matterhorn by fervent mountaineer Edward Whymper in 1865 and then the discovery of Switzerland's untouched mountain areas by British tourists caused local inhabitants to make some changes. Mountain villages were transformed into lofty resorts and fashionable holiday centres. Today roads, rails and lifts open valleys and heights. Massive dams bear witness to the importance of hydraulic power for the country's energy. European trade flows through the Alpine tunnels. But in spite of their economic development, the Swiss abide by one hard-and-fast rule: the preservation of their natural habitat in all its beauty—for without this, there would be no Switzerland.

Les montagnes

La Suisse existerait-elle sans ses montagnes? Difficile à imaginer! Depuis les temps les plus reculés, des marchands, des soldats et des voyageurs franchirent les Alpes, cette imposante barrière entre le nord et le sud de l'Europe. Les éléphants d'Hannibal et les armées de Napoléon empruntèrent les pénibles sentiers escarpés en direction de l'Italie. Un état suisse autonome n'aurait sans doute jamais existé sans les vallées alpines servant de refuge et de source de revenus. Les montagnes pourtant parurent toujours menaçantes aux yeux des hommes. Nombre de légendes racontent l'effroi face aux forces naturelles puissantes et maléfiques: on parle d'éboulements, d'avalanches, de tempêtes et de démons. Mais l'ascension spectaculaire du Cervin par le fougueux alpiniste anglais Edward Whymper en 1865 et la conquête du monde inviolé des montagnes par les touristes britanniques amenèrent les autochtones à revoir leur jugement. Les petits villages alpestres devinrent des stations climatiques d'altitude et des centres touristiques mondains. Routes, chemins de fer et funiculaires ont rendus accessibles vallées et sommets. D'imposants barrages témoignent de l'importance de la force hydraulique dans l'approvisionnement en énergie du pays. Les voies commerciales européennes passent par les tunnels alpins. Mais malgré tout, l'impératif suprême des Suisses reste: le maintien dans toute sa beauté de l'espace vital naturel car sans cela, la Suisse n'existerait pas.

山

山々なくしてスイスは存在し得るか？殆どあり得ないでしょう。太古の昔から商人が、兵士が、旅人が、ヨーロッパの南北を隔てる強大な障壁、アルプス山脈を越えて来たのです。ハンニバルの象だって、ナポレオンの軍勢も、ドイツの皇帝や詩人達も、厄介な細い山道を辿って、麓へイタリアへ、と向かったのです。アルプスの谷間が避難所として使われたり、通過交通からもたらされる収益がなかったら、スイスという独立国は存在し得なかったことでしょう。山々自体はしかし常に人間を脅かすものとして見られてきました。山の災いをもたらす圧倒的な自然の力に対する恐れを描いた伝説は数知れず。崖くずれ、雪崩、嵐や悪霊について語られています。1865年にイギリス人の登山家エドワード・ウィンパー隊が劇的なマッターホルン登頂を成し遂げ、更にイギリスからの観光客達が未踏の山の世界を「発見」するようになって初めて、地元の人々は考えを改めるようになりました。山村は高原保養地や優雅な休暇の中心地と姿を変えたのです。今日では谷も頂上も、道路や鉄道、リフトによって開発されています。重厳なダムは国のエネルギー供給に水力がいかなる意味を有するか、を示していますし、ヨーロッパ内取引の流れはアルプスのトンネルを通り抜けて行きます。しかし経済の発展にかかわらず、スイスにとっての最高位の掟は、自然にもたらされた生活空間を無傷の美しさの内に保つということです。それなしにスイスは存在し得ないのですから。

Der Aletschgletscher
ist der grösste seiner
Art in den Alpen:
24 km lang,
1800 m breit und
bis zu 800 m tief.

The Aletsch Glacier
is the longest of its
kind in the Alps:
24 km long, 1800 m
wide and
up to 800 m deep.

Le glacier d'Aletsch,
le plus important
du genre dans les
Alpes, mesure 24 km
de long, 1800 m de
large et sa profon-
deur atteint 800 m.

アルプスで同タイプ最大
のアレッチュ氷河。全長
２４ｋｍ、幅１８００ｍ、
最深８００ｍ。

Stiebende Wasser in der Aareschlucht bei Meiringen. Hier stürzte Sherlock Holmes zu Tode.

Foaming waters in the Aare Gorge near Meiringen. Sherlock Holmes fell to his death here.

Gorges de l'Aare près de Meiringen. C'est à cet endroit que Sherlock Holmes trouva la mort.

マイリンゲンのアアレ渓谷では、しぶきの飛散する水際まで細道が続く。ここでシャーロック・ホームズは転落死した。

Seilbahn auf den höchsten Aussichtsberg der Ostschweiz, den Säntis (2504 m).

The cable railway to the highest panoramic mountain in Eastern Switzerland, the Säntis (2504 m).

Le téléphérique conduisant sur le plus haut sommet à vue panoramique de la Suisse orientale, le Säntis (2504 m).

シュヴェークアルプからロープーウェイで、東スイスの最高眺望峰、センティス（2504m）へ。

Soglio, ein Bergdorf
im bündnerischen
Bergell, mit den Gip-
feln der Sciora-
Gruppe im Abend-
licht.

Soglio, a mountain
village in Bergell,
Graubunden. The
peaks of the Sciora
mountains at dusk.

Soglio, village de
montagne situé dans
la partie grisonne du
Bergell avec les som-
mets du Sciora au
coucher du soleil.

グラウビュンデン州ベル
ゲル谷の山村、ソリオ。
夕暮れ時のショーラ山脈
の峰々と。

43

Wasser
Water
L'eau
水

Der Rheinfall bei
Schaffhausen, der
grösste und imposan-
teste Wasserfall des
Kontinents.

The Rhine Falls near
Schaffhausen, the
largest and most
imposing waterfall
on the continent.

Les chutes du Rhin
près de Schaffhouse,
les plus grandes et
imposantes du conti-
nent.

ヨーロッパ大陸最大で印
象的なシャッフハウゼン
のラインの滝。

Wasser

Wasser aus der Schweiz fliesst in
vier Meere. Gebunden in Schnee
und Gletschereis, liegt es in den
Hochalpen und speist fortwährend
Rhein, Rhone und die Zuflüsse zu Donau und Po. Die Schweiz ist ein was-
serreiches Land, durchzogen von un-
zähligen Bächen und Flüssen, mal ru-
hig in kleine und grosse Seen mün-
dend, mal wild durch Schluchten
stiebend. Wasser ist der einzige
Rohstoff des Landes und wird ent-
sprechend genutzt, vor allem zur
Energiegewinnung. Hoch in den Al-
pentälern halten mächtige Talsperren das Gletscherwasser zurück, um
es dann den Turbinen der Elektrizi-
tätswerke zuzuführen. Die Wasser-
kraftwerke erzeugen über 50% des
schweizerischen Stroms. Doch Wasser braucht es auch für die Landwirt-
schaft. Auf der Alpennordseite gibt
es genügend Niederschläge, doch
auf der Südseite ist das Klima trok-
ken. Im Wallis sind kühne Bewässe-
rungsbauten zu bewundern, die
Suonen (französisch bisses), aus
Baumstämmen oder in den Fels gehauene Leitungen, die Bergbach-
wasser kilometerweit zu den dursti-
gen Feldern und Weinbergen führen. Seen und Flusslandschaften sind
aber auch Erholungsgebiete. Baden
und Wassersport sind in der
Schweiz sehr beliebt. Wie wär's mit
einem Bad in der Aare, direkt unter-
halb des Bundeshauses in Bern,
oder mit Riverrafting durch die
Rheinschlucht? Oder einfach mit einem gemütlichen Picknick an einem
idyllischen Seeufer?

Water

Water from Switzerland flows into
four seas. Bound in snow and glacial
ice, it lies in the high mountains, con-
tinuously feeding the Rhine, Rhone
and inlets to the Donau and
Po. Criss-crossed by uncountable
streams and rivers, Switzerland
abounds in water: sometimes it
quietly glides into large and small
lakes, sometimes it foams wildly
through rugged gorges. Water is
the country's only natural resource
and is used as such, primarily as a
source of energy. High up in the alpine valleys, mighty dams hold back
glacial waters used to drive the turbines of the power stations. Hydraulic power produces over 50% of
Switzerland's energy. Yet water is
also needed for agriculture. The
area north of the Alps enjoys
enough rainfall, but the south side is
dry. In the Valais bold irrigation
ducts called Suonen (bisses in
French) are cut out of tree trunks or
carved into the cliffs. They carry
water from the mountain brooks
down to the thirsty fields and vineyards kilometres away. Lakes and
riversides are also perfect recre-
ation spots. Swimming and other
water sports are very popular in
Switzerland. How about a swim in
the Aare, directly below Bern's parliament buildings, or a rousting ride
by river raft through the Rhine Falls?
Or perhaps just a peaceful picnic on
an idyllic lake-shore?

L'eau

L'eau de la Suisse se jette dans quatre mers. Figée sous forme de neige et de glace dans les Hautes Alpes, elle alimente continuellement le Rhin, le Rhône et les affluents du Danube et du Pô. La Suisse est un pays riche en eau, sillonné d'innombrables ruisseaux et rivières se jetant calmement dans de petits et grands lacs ou courant tumultueusement dans des gorges sauvages. Seule matière première du pays, l'eau est principalement utilisée à la production d'énergie. Dans les hautes vallées alpines, de puissants barrages retiennent l'eau des glaciers qui alimente ensuite les turbines des usines électriques suisses. L'agriculture est aussi tributaire de l'eau. Sur le versant nord des Alpes, les précipitations sont suffisantes tandis que sur le versant sud le climat reste sec. Dans le Valais, on peut admirer les constructions hardies de l'approvisionnement en eau appelées bisses. Ces conduites faites de demi-troncs évidés ou taillées dans le roc amènent l'eau des torrents sur des kilomètres de distance jusqu'aux champs et aux vignobles. Les régions des lacs et des rivières sont des lieux de villégiature. La natation et les sports aquatiques sont fort prisés en Suisse. Que dites-vous d'une baignade dans l'Aar, juste au-dessous du Palais fédéral à Berne, ou d'une descente en raft dans les gorges du Rhin? Ou tout simplement d'un agréable pique-nique sur la berge idyllique d'un lac?

水

水はスイスから４つの海へと流れて行きます。雪や氷河に氷結してアルプスの高地に横たわり、ライン河、ローヌ河、そしてドナウとポーの支流へと絶えず流れ込んでいるのです。スイスは水が豊かな国。そこには数知れぬほどの小川や河川が通り、時には静かに大小様々な湖へと注ぎ入り、時には荒々しく峡谷に飛び散ります。水だけがこの国が有する資源で、それ相応な扱いを受け、特にエネルギー生産のために利用されています。氷河水はアルプスの高い谷合で強大なダムに塞き止められ、発電所のタービンへ引き込まれるようになっています。スイスの電力の５０％以上が水力発電で賄われています。しかし水は発電のためだけでなく、農業にも必要です。アルプス北側では降水量は十分ですが、南側は乾燥気候。ヴァリス地方では「スオーネ」（フランス語では「ビッス」）と呼ばれる思いきった形の灌漑用水路設備に感心させられます。丸太を割り貫いたり岩を切り開いたりして作られており、山の小川の水は何キロメートルにも亙って、乾いた畑や葡萄地に運ばれます。湖や川のある風景というものは、また、憩いの場でもあります。水泳や水上スポーツはスイスでとても人気があります。ベルンの連邦議事堂のすぐ下を流れるアーレ川で泳ぐというのは如何でしょう？或いは、ライン渓谷をカヌーで下ってみては？それとも、もっと手頃に、牧歌的な湖畔での楽しいピクニック？

Rhonegletscher. Aus
der Gletscherzunge
im Oberwallis
entspringt die junge
Rhone, einer der
grossen europäi-
schen Ströme.

The Rhone Glacier.
The Rhone, one of
Europe's largest
rivers, is fed by this
glacier in the Upper
Valais.

Le glacier du Rhône.
C'est dans ce glacier
du Haut-Valais que
le Rhône, un des
grands fleuves
d'Europe, prend
sa source.

ローヌ氷河。このオーバ
ー・ヴァリスの氷河より
ヨーロッパ最大級河川ロ
ーヌが生まれる。

Skurille Steinforma-
tionen an der Ver-
zasca. Die Brücke ist
typisch für viele Tes-
siner Täler.

Bizarre rocks shaped
by the Verzasca. The
bridge is typical of
Ticino valleys.

Roches façonnées
par la Verzasca
d'une manière éton-
nante. Le pont est
typique de la région.

ヴェルツァスカ川はおか
しな形の石を造り出す。
川に掛かるはティチーノ
地方の多くの谷で典型的
な橋。

Nur zu Fuss, mit der
Bahn oder in aben-
teuerlicher Schlauch-
bootfahrt ist die
Rheinschlucht bei
Versam zugänglich.

The Rhine Gorge
near Versam is
accessible only on
foot, by rail or by an
adventurous ride on
a river raft.

Les gorges du Rhin
près de Versam ne
sont accessibles qu'à
pied, en chemin de
fer ou en «rafting»
aventureux.

ヴェルサムのライン渓谷
には、徒歩、列車、また
はスリルある渓流舟でし
か辿りつけない。

Morgenstimmung in Gandria. Von Lugano führt ein idyllischer Uferweg zu diesem malerischen Dorf.

Morning in Gandria. An idyllic lakeshore path leads from Lugano to this picturesque village.

Atmosphère matinale à Gandria. Un sentier idyllique le long du lac conduit de Lugano à ce village pittoresque.

ガンドリアの朝。情緒豊かな湖岸沿いの道が、ルガノからこの絵のような村に続く。

Reisen
Travel
Les voyages
旅行

Ein Dampfschiff auf dem Vierwaldstättersee, unterwegs nach Brunnen, das vor den markanten Felspyramiden der Mythen liegt.

A steamship on the Lake of Four Cantons, en route to Brunnen, with its backdrop of striking pyramid-shaped cliffs of the Myths.

Bateau à vapeur sur le lac des Quatre Cantons se rendant à Brunnen situé au pied des pyramides rocheuses des Mythen.

フィーアヴァルトシュテッテ（ルッツェルン）湖上の蒸気船。独特なピラミッド型岩山ミーテンの前に位置する町、ブルンネンに向かう。

Reisen

Die Schweiz ist das Land mit dem dichtesten Verkehrsnetz. Strasse und Schiene erschliessen fast jeden Winkel des Landes, und wo diese Verkehrswege unmöglich zu bauen sind – über unzugängliche Schluchten hinauf auf Alpen und Bergspitzen –, da führen Seilbahnen und Lifte hin. Die Industrialisierung der Schweiz erforderte bald einmal bessere und schnellere Verkehrswege. Nach 1850 wurde vorerst die Passstrasse über den Gotthard wintersicher ausgebaut, doch der Durchstich des Eisenbahntunnels läutete 1880 das Ende der Kutschenpost über die Alpen ein. Die Lage mitten in Europa diktierte dem jungen Staat den Ausbau von Schiene und Strasse. Dass die Schweiz nicht einfach zum Durchreiseland wurde, verdankt sie ihrer landschaftlichen Schönheit. Anfang des 20. Jahrhunderts schossen vor allem in den Alpen Kurorte und Hotels wie Pilze aus dem Boden. Die Erfindung der Zahnradbahn ermöglichte die problemlose Verbindung mit dem Talboden und machte es auch dem gebirgsunkundigsten Flachländer möglich, Gletscher und Berge von ganz nah anzuschauen. Heute ist die Schweiz stolz auf ihr fein verzweigtes öffentliches Verkehrsnetz, das kaum einen Wunsch offen lässt, sei dies im Intercity zwischen Genf und St. Gallen, im Postauto von Disentis nach Fuorns, während einer Schiffahrt auf dem Vierwaldstättersee oder hoch über den Alltagssorgen auf dem Jungfraujoch oder dem Gornergrat ob Zermatt.

Travel

Switzerland is the country with the densest traffic system. Road and rail reach almost every nook and cranny of the country, and areas where these routes cannot be built—over impenetrable gorges high in the Alps and atop mountains—are serviced by cable cars and lifts. It was not long before Switzerland's industrialisation necessitated better and faster routes. After 1850, the pass road over the Gotthard was prepared for winter crossings. Then in 1880 the railway tunnel was cut through, ringing in the end of the era of mail coaches over the Alps. Its position in the heart of Europe required the young state to expand its roads and rails. But thanks to its scenic beauty, Switzerland did not become a mere transit country. In the beginning of the 20th century resorts and hotels sprang up like mushrooms, especially in the mountains. The invention of the rack railway ensured connections between mountain and valley and enabled lowlanders, unacquainted with the ways of the mountains, to experience glaciers and peaks first hand. Today Switzerland is proud of its intricate transport system. It answers almost every wish, whether in the Intercity between Geneva and St. Gall, the postbus from Disentis to Fuorns, a ferry on the Lake of Four Cantons, or far from everyday cares atop the Jungfraujoch or Zermatt's Gornergrat.

Les voyages

La Suisse possède le réseau de communication le plus dense. La route et le rail desservent quasiment chaque recoin du pays et dans les endroits où ces voies-là ne peuvent être construites, comme par exemple au travers de gorges inaccessibles, pour atteindre alpages ou sommets montagneux, ce sont des téléfériques qui en permettent l'accès. Le développement industriel stimula le perfectionnement des voies de communication. Peu après 1850, la route du col du St-Gotthard fut améliorée pour être utilisable aussi en hiver, mais le percement du tunnel en 1880 sonna le glas de la diligence postale à travers les Alpes. La situation géographique de ce jeune état au centre de l'Europe dicta la création de routes et de voies de chemin de fer. Si la Suisse ne devint pas simplement un pays de transit, c'est grâce à la beauté de ses sites. Au début du 20e siècle et surtout dans les Alpes, les stations de villégiature et les hôtels poussèrent comme des champignons. La découverte du chemin de fer à crémaillère facilita la liaison entre la plaine et la montagne et permit aux habitants du plat pays d'admirer de près les glaciers et les rochers. Aujourd'hui, la Suisse est fière de son réseau de communications extrêmement dense qui comble tous les désirs, que ce soit l'Intercity entre Genève et St-Gall, l'autobus postal de Disentis à Fuorns, le bateau sur le Lac des Quatre Cantons ou les trains du Jungfraujoch et du Gornergrat au-dessus de Zermatt pour s'élever loin des tracas quotidiens.

旅行

スイスは交通網が大変密に張りめぐらされた国です。国内ほぼどの片隅までも道路や鉄道が行き届き、そういった交通手段の建設が不可能な、例えば人の寄りつけぬ渓谷の上だとか、アルプスや山々の頂などにはケーブルやリフトが渡されています。かつてスイスの産業化が進んだ折には、即刻、より良くより速い交通手段が必要となりました。１８５０年からまずゴットハルト峠道が冬でも通行可能なように拡張されましたが、更に１８８０年になって鉄道トンネルが貫通すると、アルプス越えの郵便馬車も終焉となりました。まだ近代連邦国家となって年の浅い国スイスにとって、そのヨーロッパの真中という土地柄、鉄道や道路の拡張は厳命でした。ところで、スイスが単に通過国とならずにすんだのは、美しい風景のお陰です。２０世紀初頭には、とりわけアルプスでは療養地やホテルがまるでキノコが土から出て来るが如く、矢継ぎ早に出現してきました。アプト式（歯軌条）鉄道が発明されると谷との連絡が問題なく行なえるようになり、山には全く不慣れな平地の住民達でも氷河や山々を間近に見ることができるようになりました。今日、綿密に枝分かれした公共交通網はスイスの誇りで、かなわぬ願いは殆どないくらい。ジュネーヴとサンクト・ガレン間はインター・シティーで、ディッセンティスからフオルンスへなら郵便バスで、フィーアヴァルトシュテッテ湖では船旅を、そして日常の煩わしさを超えた高きのユングフラウヨッホやツェルマットの上のゴルナーグラートにさえ行き着く手段があるのです。

Der Viadukt bei
Filisur, eine der kühn-
sten Bauten der Rhä-
tischen Bahnen, die
auch im Winter die
Bündner Täler ver-
binden.

The viaduct near
Filisur, one of the bol-
dest constructions of
the Rhaetic Rail, joins
the Graubunden val-
leys in winter too.

Le Viaduc de Filisur,
l'une des construc-
tions les plus auda-
cieuses des Chemins
de Fer Rhétiques qui,
même durant l'hiver,
relient les vallées des
Grisons.

フィリズールの高架橋。
冬でもグラウビュンデン
の谷々を結ぶレーティシ
ュ鉄道の大胆な建築。

Die erste Brücke über
die Schöllenen an
der Gotthardroute
soll der Teufel
gebaut haben.

Legend has it that the
Devil built the first
bridge over the
Schöllenen on the
Gotthard route.

La légende attribue
au diable la con-
struction du premier
pont enjambant la
gorge des Schöl-
lenen sur la route du
St-Gotthard.

シェレネン渓谷に掛かっ
た最初の橋は悪魔の成せ
る業と言われる。昔ゴッ
タルトを越えたい者はこ
こを通らねばならなかっ
た。

Die Jungfraubahn mit
Eiger und Mönch.

The Jungfrau Rail,
Eiger and Mönch.

Le chemin de fer de
la Jungfrau avec
l'Eiger et le Mönch.

クライネン・シャイデッ
クのユングフラウ鉄道。
ここからアイガー北壁を
抜けて、ユングフラウヨ
ッホへ登る。

Die Schilthornbahn
hievt die Feriengäste
im Nu aus dem
Nebel, mitten in die
majestätische Berner
Alpenwelt.

The Schilthorn Rail
lifts visitors out of the
fog and into the
heart of the majestic
Bernese Alps.

Le téléphérique du
Schilthorn emporte
les touristes en un
rien de temps hors du
brouillard jusqu'au
milieu du monde
majestueux des
Alpes bernoises.

シールトホルン・バーン
は、あっと言う間に、休
暇客を霧の中から堂々た
るベルナーアルプスの世
界へ引き揚げてくれる。

**Ausflugsziele
Destinations
Buts d'excursions
行楽先**

Hoch über Luzern und dem Vierwaldstättersee liegt der Gipfel des Pilatus. Der Blick schweift weit über die Innerschweiz.

The Pilatus towers high above Lucerne and the Lake of Four Cantons. The view stretches as far as Central Switzerland.

Depuis le sommet du Pilate au-dessus de Lucerne et du lac des Quatre Cantons, le regard embrasse une vaste partie de la Suisse centrale.

ルッツェルンやフィーア ヴァルトシュテッテ湖の 遥か上方にあるピラトゥ ス山頂上。眺望は中央ス イスに広がる。

Ausflugsziele

Die Schweiz ist ein Europa im Kleinen. Die Wege zu den vielen Sehenswürdigkeiten sind kurz. Innerhalb eines Tages fährt man bequem vom Rheinfall oder der Zürcher Bahnhofstrasse, vorbei an lieblichen Seen, über kühn angelegte Passstrassen ins mediterrane Tessin oder durch das von vielen malerischen Kleinstädten geprägte Mittelland an die rebengesäumten Ufer des Genfersees. Der kulturgeschichtlich Interessierte findet Zeugen aller Epochen: Ruinen der Römerstädte Avenches und Augst, die romanische Kirche Romainmôtier, die gotischen Münster von Fribourg und Bern, die barocken Klosteranlagen St. Gallen und Einsiedeln. Burgen und Schlösser überschauen weite und enge Täler, als ob die Ritter und Räuber heute noch dort wohnten. Die bäuerliche Tradition der Schweiz ist vielerorts sichtbar: im Freilichtmuseum Ballenberg, das Bauernhäuser aus allen Regionen zeigt, beim nachfolgenden Besuch bei einem Brienzer Holzschnitzer oder im hautnahen Miterleben der Käseherstellung in den Schaukäsereien Gruyères oder Stein bei Appenzell. Wer eher technisch interessiert ist, fährt ins Verkehrshaus Luzern, ins Technorama Winterthur, ins Uhrenmuseum in La Chaux-de-Fonds oder kann vor einem der imposanten Staudämme ins Staunen geraten. Die Schweiz im Taschenformat gibt es in Melide am Luganersee zu bestaunen: bedeutende Bauwerke als Modelle, dicht beieinander.

Destinations

Switzerland is Europe in miniature. Distances to the many sights are short. Take the trip from the Rhine Falls for example, or Zurich's Bahnhofstrasse. Travel past charming lakes and over bold pass roads into Mediterranean Ticino. Or through the Mittelland, dotted with picturesque little towns, to the vineyards on Lake Geneva's shores. Each trip is a comfortable day's journey. Anyone interested in the history of civilization will find traces of every epoch: ruins of the Roman cities of Avenches and Augst, the Romanesque church in Romainmôtier, the Gothic cathedrals of Fribourg and Bern, baroque monasteries in St. Gall and Einsiedeln. Fortresses and castles guard the valleys, as if knights and bandits still lived there. Switzerland's rustic tradition is also apparent in many places: in the open-air museum of Ballenberg, where farmhouses from all regions are on display. Visit a Brienz woodcarver, or get first-hand experience of cheese-making in the dairies in Gruyères or Stein by Appenzell. If your interests are of a more technical bent, there's the Transport Museum in Lucerne, Winterthur's Technorama, the Watch Museum in La Chaux-de-Fonds, or an imposing dam. In Melide on Lake Lugano you can admire a Switzerland of pocketbook size, where models of important buildings are displayed close together.

Buts d'excursions

La Suisse est l'Europe en petit. Les distances entre les choses intéressantes à voir sont courtes. Depuis les chutes du Rhin ou la Bahnhofstrasse de Zurich, on peut aisément gagner en un jour le Tessin méditerranéen en longeant des lacs ravissants et en empruntant des routes audacieuses pour franchir les cols. De même il est aisé de traverser le Moyen-Pays aux nombreuses petites villes pittoresques pour atteindre les vignobles des bords du Léman. L'amateur de culture et d'histoire peut trouver en Suisse des témoignages de toutes les époques: les ruines romaines des cités d'Avenches et d'Augst, l'église romane de Romainmôtier, les cathédrales gothiques de Fribourg et de Berne, les monastères baroques de St-Gall et d'Einsiedeln. Forteresses et châteaux sont les sentinelles d'étroites ou larges vallées. La tradition paysanne suisse est visible en maints endroits: au musée en plein air de Ballenberg avec ses maisons rurales de toutes les régions du pays, chez un sculpteur sur bois de Brienz ou dans les fromageries de démonstration à Gruyères ou à Stein près d'Appenzell. Celui qui s'intéresse à la technique peut aller au musée des transports à Lucerne, au Technorama de Winterthour, au musée de l'horlogerie à la Chaux-de-Fonds ou admirer les digues imposantes des barrages. La Suisse en miniature se trouve à Melide au bord du lac de Lugano: des bâtiments en modèles réduits, caractéristiques de toute la Suisse, s'y côtoient.

行楽先

スイスは小型のヨーロッパ。多くの名所へすぐに行けます。ラインの滝やチューリッヒのバーンホーフ通りを出発して、奇麗な湖畔を通り大胆に切り開かれた峠道を越えて地中海風なティチーノにも、また、絵のように美しいたくさんの小さな村に形造られたミッテルランドを通って葡萄畑に縁どられたレマン湖岸にも、一日の内に便利快適に行きつけます。文化的・歴史的な面に興味があれば、アヴァンシュやアウグストの古代ローマ時代の町の遺跡、ローマ様式の教会ロマンモティエー、フリブールやベルンのゴシック様式大寺院、サンクト・ガレンやアインシーデルンのバロック様式修道院など、あらゆる時代の立ち会い人に出合うことができます。砦や城は今でも騎士や盗賊が住むかの如く、遠く狭い谷合を見張っています。また、スイス農家の伝統はあちこちで見られます。バレンベルク屋外博物館ではあらゆる地方の農家を展示していますし、ブリエンツの木彫り師を訪ねたり、グルイエールやアッペンツェル州のシュタインではチーズ作りを実体験することもできます。技術面により興味を持つなら、ルッツェルンの交通博物館やヴィンタートゥールのテクノラマ、ラ・ショー・ド・フォンの時計博物館へも行ってみますし、堂々たるダムの一つを訪れその驚異を学ぶこともできるでしょう。ルガノ湖畔のメリーデには吃驚するようなスイスのミニアチュアがあり、有名な建物の模型がぎっしり立ち並んでいます。

Einsiedeln, vor allem
die Gnadenkapelle
mit der schwarzen
Madonna, ist der
bedeutendste
schweizerische
Wallfahrtsort.

Einsiedeln, with its
Grace Chapel and
Black Madonna, is
the most significant
destination in
Switzerland for
pilgrims.

Einsiedeln, et surtout
sa Chapelle de la
Grâce avec la
Madone noire, est le
lieu de pèlerinage
le plus important
de Suisse.

アインシーデルン、とり
わけ黒きマドンナの坐す
聖母チャペルはスイスの
重要な巡礼地。

Im Freilichtmuseum Ballenberg bei Brienz sind Bauernhäuser aus der ganzen Schweiz vereint.

Farm houses from all over Switzerland are brought together in the Ballenberg Open Air Museum near Brienz.

Le musée en plein air de Ballenberg près de Brienz réunit les maisons rurales de toute la Suisse.

ブリエンツ近郊のバレンベルク屋外博物館には、農家や芸術手工芸品がスイス全国から集められている。

Das Kleinstädtchen Gruyères. In der Schaukäserei wird die Käseherstellung vorgeführt.

The little town Gruyères. The dairy carries out demonstrations of cheesemaking for the public.

La petite ville de Gruyères. A la fromagerie de démonstration on peut suivre la fabrication du fromage.

岩の先端に立つ小さな町グルイエール。チーズ製造工程を見せる、見学用チーズ製造所がある。

70

Guarda ist eines der
schönsten Unter-
engadiner Dörfer.
Die Hausfassaden
sind reich mit Sgraffiti
verziert.

Guarda is one of the
most beautiful
villages in the Lower
Engadine: house
façades with their
decorative inscrip-
tions.

Guarda, l'un des
plus beaux villages
de la Basse Enga-
dine. Les façades de
ses maisons sont
richement décorées
de graffitis.

ウンター・エンガディン
で最も美しい村の一つ、
グアルダ。家の正面はス
グラッフィッティ模様で
装飾されている。

Brauchtum
Customs
Coutumes
風俗

Alpaufzug, ein spezieller Tag für die Sennen. Für einige Zeit können die Tiere nun auf den saftigen Alpweiden grasen.

This is a special day for the dairy farmers, whose animals can now graze in lush alpine meadows.

La montée à l'alpage, un jour particulier pour les armaillis du Toggenbourg. Le bétail pourra brouter quelque temps l'herbe savoureuse des pâturages.

酪農家にとって特別な日、アルプアウフツーク。これから暫く動物達は柔らかなアルプスの草原で草を食むことができる。

Brauchtum

Wenn der Appenzeller Senn nicht nur die goldene Kuh am Ohr trägt, sondern auch seine gelb und rot leuchtende Sonntagstracht anzieht, dann ist für ihn ein besonderer Tag: Alpaufzug. Er führt die Kühe zur Sömmerung auf die Alp, lebt dort allein, umgeben von Glockengebimmel und freier Natur. Wenn er laut den Alpgruss singt, macht er das aus Lebensfreude und Gott zum Dank. Das Brauchtum ist in der ländlichen Bevölkerung der Schweiz noch immer stark verwurzelt. Alphornblasen und Fahnenschwingen, Ländlermusik und *Chästeilet* sind echter Ausdruck der alten Volkskultur und nicht eine Show für Touristen. Sichtbare Zeichen des Kulturguts sind die Wohnhäuser: die behäbigen Stadthäuser der Bürger und die mit Schnitzereien und Blumen geschmückten Bauernhäuser. Die Formen unterscheiden sich von Region zu Region, sind geprägt von Natur und Landschaft, die ihrerseits den Menschenschlag im jeweiligen Gebiet beeinflussen. Auch Feste gehören zum Brauchtum.. In den katholischen Kantonen ziehen die Gläubigen an Festtagen in farbenprächtigen Prozessionen durchs Dorf und übers Land. Kaum sind die Trauben geerntet, feiern Westschweizer und Tessiner den neuen Weinjahrgang in ausgelassenen *Fêtes des Vendanges*. Und wenn Fasnacht ist, vertreiben die Narren auch die allerbösesten Geister mit Trommeln, falschen Tönen und furchterregenden Masken – besonders lautstark in Basel und Luzern.

Customs

When the Appenzell farmer puts on his golden cow earring and dons his bright red and yellow traditional Sunday garb, it's a special day: time for the alpine procession, when he leads his cows to their mountain pastures. And there he lives alone, amid the clanging of bells and nature. His loud *Alpine Greeting* is sung to show his joy of living and to thank God. This custom is still deeply rooted among Switzerland's rural population. Alphorn and flag-swinging, ländlermusic and the *Chästeilet,* a traditional festival, when the summer's cheese is distributed, are genuine expressions of ancient folklore and not tourist shows. These cultural values are evident in the houses: sedate town homes and proud farmhouses, with their intricate wood carvings and bright flowers. Their shapes, differing from region to region, reflect nature and the landscape, which in turn influence the people. Festivities are also traditional. On religious holidays in Catholic cantons, believers march through land and village in colourful processions. When the grapes have barely been harvested, West Swiss and Ticinese celebrate next year's wine with boisterous *Fêtes des Vendanges*. And during *Fasnacht* "fools" drive out evil spirits with drums, jarring music and frightening masks—with particular success in Basel and Lucerne.

Coutumes

Lorsque le vacher appenzellois revêt son lumineux costume du dimanche jaune et rouge en plus de la vache d'or qu'il porte à l'oreille, c'est qu'il vit un jour particulier: la montée à l'alpage. Il va conduire les vaches en estivage dans les hauts pâturages. Il reste seul là-haut, entouré du bruit des sonnailles dans la belle nature sauvage. Lorsqu'il chante à pleine voix le salut à l'alpe, il exprime sa joie de vivre et remercie Dieu. Les traditions sont encore fortement ancrées dans la population rurale suisse. Le cor des Alpes, le lancer du drapeau, la musique folklorique et la fête de la pesée des fromages sont l'expression d'une vieille culture populaire et non pas un spectacle pour touristes. Les maisons sont les témoignages visibles du patrimoine culturel telles les opulentes demeures citadines des bourgeois ou les fermes aux façades décorées de reliefs et de fleurs. Les types de construction changent d'une région à l'autre en fonction de la nature et de l'environnement. Les fêtes aussi font partie des coutumes. Dans les cantons catholiques, lors des célébrations religieuses, les fidèles défilent en processions hautes en couleurs à travers villages et campagnes. En Suisse romande et au Tessin, la récolte du raisin à peine achevée, on célèbre le nouveau millésime par de joyeuses fêtes des vendanges. Au moment du carnaval, on chasse les mauvais esprits au moyen de tambours, de fausses notes et de masques effrayants. Le carnaval de Bâle et celui de Lucerne ont un éclat tout particulier.

風俗

アッペンツェルの酪農家の男が金の牛の耳飾りを付けているだけでなく、黄と赤に輝く日曜日の衣裳を身に付けているとすれば、その日は彼にとって特別な日、アルプアウフツーク（アルプ－高原牧場－に登る日）。牛を連れてアルプに登り、そこで絶え間ない牛鐘の音と広々とした自然に囲まれて、一人で一夏を過ごします。アルプグルス（アルプへの挨拶）を大声で歌えば、それは生きる喜びと神への感謝を表すものです。スイスの田舎の住民の間では風俗習慣が今尚根強く残っています。アルペンホルン吹奏やファーネンシュヴィンゲン（旗を用いる演技）、レントラー音楽、ケーズタイレット（チーズの祭）は単なる観光客向けのショーではなく古い民俗文化に基づく本物です。目に見える文化財には家があります。市民達のしっかりとした町の家や、彫刻や花に飾られた農家。形は地方毎に異なり、その土地の人間に影響を与える自然と風景に仕上げられています。祭もまた風俗の一つ。カソリックのカントン（州）では祝日には信者達が色華やかに村や田園をパレードします。西スイスやティチーノでは、新しいワインの年を賑やかなワイン祭で祝わずに葡萄を収穫する、などということは殆どあり得ません。そしてファスナハト（カーニバル）となると、仮装した幾つものグループが狂った音色や恐ろしい仮面でどんな酷い悪魔でも追い払ってしまいます。バーゼルとルッツェルンではとりわけ大きな成功が収められています。

In Kippel im Löt-
schental geben die
«Herrgottsgrena-
diere» der Fronleich-
namsprozession ihr
farbenprächtiges
Geleit.

The "Lord's Grena-
diers" add their col-
ourful touch to the
Corpus Christi Pro-
cession in Kippel, Löt-
schental.

A Kippel au Löt-
schental les «Grena-
diers du Seigneur»
mettent une touche
colorée à la proces-
sion de la Fête-Dieu.

レッチェン谷のキッペル
では聖体節の行列に「ヘ
ルゴッツグレナディーレ」
（神の選抜歩兵隊）が豊
かな彩りを添える。

Das Schwingen ist für die ländliche Bevölkerung der Schweiz Nationalsport.

Swiss wrestling, or "Schwingen", is Swiss country folk's national sport and always a good reason to celebrate.

La lutte est un sport national pour la population campagnarde et donne lieu à des festivités.

シュヴィンゲンはスイスの田舎の人々にとって国民的スポーツ。祭の好機会となる。

Chästeilet. Der auf der Alp hergestellte Käse wird – wie hier im Justistal – verteilt und verkauft.

Distributing the cheese. Cheese produced in the alps – as here in Justistal – is divided and sold.

La pesée du fromage. Le fromage fait artisanalement à l'alpage – ici au Justistal – est distribué et vendu.

ケーゼタイレット。こちらユスティス谷でのように、アルプで作られたチーズは一日の内に分けて販売される。

Narrentreiben an
der Basler Fasnacht.
Um 4 Uhr morgens
geht es hier mit dem
Zapfenstreich
gewaltig und laut-
stark los!

Driving out the fools
at the Basel Fas-
nacht. At the stroke
of 4 in the morning,
celebrations get off
with a veritable
bang.

Masques au Car-
naval de Bâle.
A 4 heures du matin
le «Zapfenstreich»
donne bruyamment
le signal de départ
du grand branle-bas.

バーゼルのカーニバルで
の仮装騒ぎ。早朝4時の
合図で、カー杯騒々しく
始まる。

Das Bundeshaus in
Bern. Im November
findet jeweils der
«Zibelemärit» statt,
ein ganz der Zwiebel
gewidmetes Fest.

The Parliament Build-
ings in Bern. The
''Onion Market'' is
held every
November, a festival
devoted entirely to
onions.

Le Palais Fédéral de
Berne. En novembre
a lieu le marché aux
oignons (Zibele-
märit), une fête entiè-
rement dédiée à
l'oignon.

ベルンの連邦議事堂前の
広場では11月毎に「ツ
ィーベルメリトゥ」と呼
ばれる、タマネギの祭、
タマネギ大市が開かれる。

Geschichte
History
Histoire
歴史

Geschichte

1991 hat die Schweiz ihren 700. Geburtstag gefeiert. Schon im Mittelalter reifte ein besonderer Sinn für Freiheit und Unabhängigkeit in den Bewohnern der Alpentäler. Dem Teufel haben die pfiffigen Urner mit einem Geissbock ein Schnippchen geschlagen, und Wilhelm Tell, der den kaiserlichen Landvogt gar nicht mochte, erschoss diesen mit der Armbrust. Zwar sind dies nur Sagen, doch sie erzählen in einfachen Worten vom Kampf der Eidgenossen gegen Bevormundung. Einzig Napoleon gelang es, die älteste Republik der Welt für kurze Zeit zu besetzen.

Das Gebiet der Schweiz wurde 1848 zu einem modernen Bundesstaat. Doch lange vor der Gründung der Eidgenossenschaft 1291 war es ein bedeutendes europäisches Kulturland. Die Römer legten die ersten Passstrassen an und ruhten sich in den warmen Quellen aus. Das Kloster St. Gallen war im Hochmittelalter *die* Adresse für Gelehrsamkeit und Bildung. Basel errichtete eine der ersten Universitäten Europas, und in Genf fanden Calvin und Rousseau das Umfeld, das sie zu ihren philosophischen und gesellschaftlichen Forderungen führte. 1864 gründet Henri Dunant das Rote Kreuz, die Schweiz finanziert und organisiert seine weltweite humanitäre Tätigkeit. Heute beschäftigt die Schweizer die Frage, ob sie die in 700 Jahren liebgewonnene Unabhängigkeit zugunsten der Integration in Europa teilweise aufgeben wollen.

History

In 1991 Switzerland celebrated its 700th anniversary. The inhabitants of the alpine valleys were developing their special sense of freedom and independence way back in the Middle Ages. The clever people of Uri outfoxed the devil with a billy-goat and William Tell, who had a great dislike for the imperial bailiff, shot him with his crossbow. These are merely legends, yet in simple words they tell the tale of the Confederates in their battle against patronage. Only Napoleon managed to briefly occupy the world's oldest republic. The area of Switzerland became a modern Federal State in 1848. Yet long before Confederation in 1291, it was an important centre of European civilization. The Romans built the first pass roads and lazed in the country's thermal springs. The monastery in St. Gall was *the* institute for higher learning and education in the Middle Ages. Basel established one of the first universities in Europe and Calvin's and Rousseau's philosophical and social demands fell on fertile ground in Geneva. In 1864 Henri Dunant founded the Red Cross, and Switzerland finances and organises its worldwide humanitarian activities. The question concerning the Swiss today is whether they want to give up their cherished, 700-year-old independence, for the sake of an integrated Europe.

Histoire

En 1991, la Suisse a fêté son 700ème anniversaire. Au Moyen Age déjà mûrissait chez les habitants des vallées alpestres ce sens tout particulier de liberté et d'indépendance. Les uranais rusés firent la nique au diable avec un bouc et Guillaume Tell, qui ne pouvait souffrir le bailli impérial, abattit ce dernier au moyen de son arbalète. Certes ce ne sont que des légendes, mais elles témoignent en termes simples de la lutte des Confédérés contre toute tutelle. Seul Napoléon parvint à occuper, pour une courte durée, la plus vieille république du monde. La Suisse devint en 1848 un état confédéré moderne. Bien avant la fondation de la Confédération en 1291, elle était un pays européen important et cultivé. Les Romains établirent les premières routes de cols et surent se détendre dans les sources thermales. Le monastère de St-Gall était au Haut Moyen Age le lieu par excellence de l'érudition et de la culture. Bâle édifia l'une des premières universités d'Europe et à Genève, Calvin et Rousseau trouvèrent l'environnement propice à leurs quêtes philosophique et sociale. Henri Dunant fonda en 1864 la Croix Rouge et la Suisse finance et organise une activité humanitaire sur le plan mondial. Aujourd'hui les Suisses sont préoccupés par la question de savoir s'ils veulent renoncer partiellement à leur indépendance, qui leur est devenue chère au cours des 700 ans écoulés, au profit de l'intégration à l'Europe.

歴史

１９９１年にスイスは建国７００周年を祝いました。既に中世紀にアルプスの谷の住民の間には自由と独立に対する特別な感覚が発達していたのです。気転のきくウリ人達は雄ヤギを使ってうまく悪魔のもくろみを壊し、威張った代官が気に入らないヴィルヘルム・テルは、アルムブルスト（いし弓）で彼を射る覚悟でした。これらは伝説でしかありませんが、スイス国民の支配者に対する戦いを簡単な言葉で綴ったものなのです。ナポレオンだけが短期間ながら世界最古の共和国を支配下に収めたことがあります。

スイス地域は１８４８年に近代的な連邦国になりましたが、そのスイス連邦創設のずっと以前、１２９１年に既に重要なヨーロッパ文化国の一つでした。古代ローマ人は最初の峠道を建設し、温泉で疲れを癒しました。サンクト・ガレンの修道院は中世の最盛期には世に知れた教養・学識の場でしたし、バーゼルにはヨーロッパでは草分けの一つとして大学が創立され、また、カルヴィンやルソーは自らの哲学や社会的要求に帰着する環境をジュネーヴに見い出しています。１８６４年にアンリ・デュナンが赤十字を設立し、スイスはその世界に広がる人道的活動を財政援助し運営しています。さて、この７００年に亙って愛着してきた独立をヨーロッパ統合の為に一部放棄したいのかどうか。スイス人は今日この問いと取り組んでいます。

Avenches, früher
Aventicum, war zur
Römerzeit die
bedeutendste und
grösste Stadt Helve-
tiens, mit Thermen
und Theatern.

Avenches, known
earlier as Aventicum,
was the largest and
most important city in
Helvetia during the
Roman era, with
thermal baths and
theatres.

Avenches – Aven-
ticum au temps des
romains – était la
ville la plus impor-
tante de l'Helvétie,
avec ses thermes et
ses théâtres.

アヴァンシュ（旧アヴェ
ンティクム）は古代ロー
マ時代にはヘルヴェティ
アの最重要・最大都市で、
温泉や劇場があった。

Das Telldenkmal in Altdorf erinnert an die legendenumwobene Gründungsgeschichte der Eidgenossenschaft.

The Tell Monument in Altdorf is a reminder of the legends of the founding of the Swiss Confederation.

Le monument de Tell à Altdorf nous rappelle l'histoire légendaire de la création de notre Confédération.

アルトドルフのテル記念碑。伝説が纏る連邦の建国話が思い起こされる。

Romainmôtier, das bedeutendste romanische Bauwerk der Schweiz.

Romainmôtier, the most important Romanesque construction in Switzerland.

Romainmôtier, le bâtiment roman le plus important de Suisse.

ロマンモティエ。旧修道院教会はスイスの最重要古代ローマ建築である。

Der barocke Prachts-
saal der Stiftsbiblio-
thek von St. Gallen
birgt wertvollste früh-
mittelalterliche
Handschriften.

The magnificent
baroque hall of the
St. Gall Foundation
Library contains
invaluable manu-
scripts dating back
to the early Middle
Ages.

La somptueuse salle
baroque de la biblio-
thèque conventuelle
de St-Gall contient
de précieux manus-
crits du Haut Moyen
Age.

サンクト・ガレンの修道
院図書館の豪華なバロッ
ク様式広間には、価値あ
る中世初期の手記が保存
されている。

Die Schweiz in Zahlen		Switzerland in Figures	
Land		**Country**	
Fläche	41 293 km²	Area	41 293 km²
Alpen	65%	Alps	65%
Mittelland	25%	Mittelland	25%
Jura	10%	Jura	10%
Landwirtschaftlich nutzbar	26%	Arable Land	26%
Höchster Punkt:		Highest point:	
Dufourspitze	4634 m ü. M.	Dufourspitze	4634 m
Tiefster Punkt:		Lowest point:	
Lago Maggiore	193 m ü. M.	Lake Maggiore	193 m
Bevölkerung (Zahlen 1990)		**People** (Figures of 1990)	
Wohnbevölkerung	6 751 000	Population	6 751 000
Ausländer	1 126 000	Foreigners	1 126 000
Volksdichte	164/km²	Population density	164/km²
Erwerbstätige	3 519 000	Number employed	3 519 000
in Landwirtschaft	197 000	in agriculture	197 000
in Industrie	1 235 000	in industry	1 235 000
in Dienstleistungen	2 087 000	in services	2 087 000
Sprachen		Languages	
deutsch	65%	German	65%
französisch	18%	French	18%
italienisch	10%	Italian	10%
rätoromanisch	1%	Rhaeto-Romanic	1%
übrige	6%	Other	6%
Wirtschaft (1990)		**Economy** (Figures of 1990)	
Bruttoinlandprodukt	317 Mrd. sFr.	Gross national product	Sfr. 317 Bill.
pro Kopf	46 600 sFr.	per person	Sfr. 46,600
Volkseinkommen	266 Mrd. sFr.		
Export	115 Mrd. sFr.	Export	Sfr. 115 Bill.
Import	113 Mrd. sFr.	Import	Sfr. 113 Bill.

Wichtigste Sektoren: Maschinen, Uhren, Chemie, Nahrungsmittel, Banken, Versicherungen, Tourismus

Major sectors: machines, watches, chemicals, foodstuffs, banks, insurances, tourism

Politik

Bundesstaat mit 26 Kantonen
Regierung: 7 Bundesräte
Parlament: Nationalrat (200 Volksvertreter); Ständerat (46 Kantonsvertreter)
Hauptstadt: Bern

Politics

Federal State with 26 cantons
Government: 7 Federal Councillors
Parliament: National Council (200 representatives of the people); Council of States (46 representatives of the cantons)
Capital city: Bern

La Suisse en chiffres

Le pays
Surface	41 293 km²
Les Alpes	65%
Le Moyen-pays	25%
Le Jura	10%
Terres agricoles	26%
Point culminant:	
Pointe Dufour	4634 m
Point le plus bas:	
Lac Majeur	193 m

Population (chiffres de 1990)
Autochtones	6 751 000
Étrangers	1 126 000
Densité de la population	164/km²
Population active	3 519 000
dans l'agriculture	197 000
dans l'industrie	1 235 000
dans les services	2 087 000
Langues	
allemand	65%
français	18%
italien	10%
romanche	1%
autres	6%

Economie (1990)
Produit national brut	317 Mrd. frs.
par habitant	46 600 frs.
Revenu national	266 Mrd. frs.
Exportations	115 Mrd. frs.
Importations	113 Mrd. frs.

Secteurs les plus importants:
machines, montres, chimie,
produits alimentaires, banques,
assurances, tourisme

Politique
Confédération de 26 cantons
Gouvernement: 7 Conseillers
Fédéraux
Parlement: Conseil national (200
représent. du peuple); Conseil des
Etats (46 représent. des cantons)
Capitale: Berne

数字で見たスイス

国土
面積：	41'293 km²
アルプス：	65 %
ミッテルランド：	25 %
ユラ：	10 %
耕作可能地：	26 %
最高地点：デュフル峰	4634 m
最低地点：マジョレー湖	193 m

人
居住者：	6'751'000
外国人：	1'126'000
人口密度：	164 / km²
勤労者：	3'519'000
農業：	197'000
工業：	1'235'000
サービス：	2'087'000
言語：ドイツ語	65 %
フランス語	18 %
イタリア語	10 %
レートロマンシュ語	1 %
その他	6 %

経済 (1990)
国内総生産：	3170 億 sFr
一人頭：	46'600 sFr
国民所得：	2660 億 sFr
輸出：	1150 億 sFr
輸入：	1130 億 sFr

重要部門：機械、時計、化学、食品、銀行、
保険、観光

政治
２６州（カントン）から成る
連邦国政府：大臣７名
国会：国民議会（国民代表200名）
全州議会（州代表46名）
首都：ベルン

© 1992
AT Verlag Aarau/Schweiz
Text und Konzept: Patrick Werschler, Bolligen

Bilder:
W. Imber, Günsberg (Seite 10,18/19, 21, 22/23, 34/35,
38/39, 44/45, 48/49, 52/53, 58/59, 60, 62/63, 72/73,
78/79, 82/83, 84/85)
M. Niederhauser, Bremgarten (Seite 8/9, 11, 12/13, 14/15,
28/29, 31, 42/43, 51, 68/69, 80, 81, 90, 91, 92/93)
F. Rausser, Bolligen (Seite 4/5, 30, 32/33, 74/75)
Christof Sonderegger, Rheineck (Seite 41, 61, 64/65, 88/89)
H. Anderegg, Ennetmoos (Seite 24/25, 50, 54/55)
Peter Studer, Grosshöchstetten (Buchumschlag sowie
Seite 40)
Heinz Dietz, Merlischachen (Seite 20, 71)
Rudolf Hunziker, (Seite 70)

Übersetzung:
Englisch: Monty Sufrin, Münsingen
Französisch: Carmen Scherrer, Château-d'Œx
Japanisch: Urs und Tamami Loosli, Zürich

Satz, Lithos und Druck: Grafische Betriebe
Aargauer Tagblatt AG, Aarau
Bindearbeiten: Buchbinderei Schumacher, Schmitten
Printed in Switzerland

ISBN 3-85502-449-9

Massstab 1:1 250 000